D0264800

ONE GINGER PELÉ!

FOOTBALL'S FUNNIEST SONGS AND CHANTS

CHRIS PARKER

This edition first published in 2008 by New Holland Publishers (UK) Ltd
London • Cape Town • Sydney • Auckland
www.newhollandpublishers.com

10 9 8 7 6 5 4 3 2 1

Garfield House, 86–88 Edgware Road, London, W2 2EA, United Kingdom
80 McKenzie Street, Cape Town, 8001, South Africa
Unit 1, 66 Gibbes Street, Chatswood, NSW 2067, Australia
218 Lake Road, Northcote, Auckland, New Zealand

ISBN 978 1 84773 252 1

Senior Editor: Kate Parker
Publishing Director: Rosemary Wilkinson
Cover design and design: Vanessa Green
Production: Melanie Dowland

Reproduction by Pica Digital PTE Ltd, Singapore
Printed and bound by C & C Offset Printing Co Ltd, China

CONTENTS

I'VE ALWAYS LOVED the atmosphere of a football match. The banter between friends in the local pubs and cafés, the sense of anticipation as you walk to the ground, the grease in your belly from that burger-van heart attack in a bun. Then there's the ritual of buying your programme, the squeeze through the turnstile and the wave of sound that hits you as you walk up the steps and emerge from the depths of the stadium out onto the stands.

As a boy, going with my dad to watch the football, match day was an assault on all the senses – but it's the noise of the crowd that I remember most. That and the sense of unity, of belonging to a group with one joint cause: to sing your hearts out and support your team. And that is the reason why, every weekend, over a million people across the length and breadth of the country turn up and sing – they're doing their bit for their team.

But while the basic reason for singing might be quite simple, the songs themselves are often very clever: satirical, witty, sometimes absurd, and, most importantly, downright funny; if you were to look for a modern-day poet you could do a lot worse than start at your local football ground. Poet Laureate, Andrew Motion has even described the body of football songs in the country as a 'huge reservoir of folk poetry' (although as an Arsenal fan, I'm not sure he's qualified to comment!).

That said, we all know that not all football fans are Shakespeares in the making and not every song is a carefully crafted sonnet designed to give some encouragement to those 11 lads trying their damndest. In fact, the best football chants are often quite offensive, and that is where much of the humour lies. We sarcastically take pleasure in the other side's misfortunes because we know that the shoe will, at some point, be firmly on the other foot. So we enjoy it while we can. And if we're only rarely in the position of gloating over the opposition, then there's always self-deprecating realism to fall back on – just look at the Gillingham supporters happily singing 'We're shit and we know we are!'

Not only are the songs often very cleverly constructed, they're also extremely informative. Football chants give a running commentary on the game, the goings-on both on and off the pitch and, more often than not, an insight into the popular culture and events of the time. They're often a spontaneous reaction to what's going on and it's a good bet that, if you were to listen to the songs sung at a game without any knowledge of how the match panned out, you'd be able to work out the score, the scorers, the players who played well, those who didn't, and what had been happening in the world in recent days... all from a few chants!

What's also incredible is that no one teaches the crowd the chants. You're not handed a song sheet on your way into the ground and the words aren't put up on the big screen with a

helpful bouncing ball to guide you through, yet thousands of fans manage to sing in unison to often completely new chants. I suppose they just start from somewhere within the crowd and grow. Or if they're no good they quickly die out – the principle of natural selection in action!

While crowds up and down the country have done a lot of the selecting for me, I've also spent hours reading through songs and chants that fans from many clubs have kindly sent in. There are hundreds to choose from, so my selection has been based on one main criterion: the song had to be funny. I've omitted racist or overly offensive chants because they're not amusing and, thankfully, those who sing them are part of a dying breed. But I've not shirked from those that come close to crossing the bad-taste line – as long as they're funny then they're in (Grandma, please stop reading at this point!).

So I hope that in the book you'll find songs to make you chuckle, chants by your team that you read with pride, and songs to remember and tell your mates. Most of all, I hope you enjoy reading this book as much as I've enjoyed writing it.

YOUR FAVOURITE PLAYERS

Every fan has a player that he or she idolizes, whether it's a French winger with long flowing locks and silky skills to match, or the scarred centre-back who has been a stalwart in your team for the past ten years. And what better way to show your love and appreciation for them than by singing their very own song?

Manchester United fans sing about their favourite goalkeeper and their belief that he has Tourettes Syndrome: (♫ 'Chim Chim Cher-ee')

Tim Timminy
Tim Timminy
Tim Tim Tirooo
We've got Tim Howard
And he says 'fuck you!'

No song about Gary Neville would be complete without reference to his imaginatively named father: (♫ 'Rebel Rebel')

Neville Neville, you play in defence
Neville Neville, your play is immense
Neville Neville, like Jacko you're bad
Neville Neville is the name of your dad!

But Gary and Neville are only part of the family. Despite a move from United to Everton, Phil remains a firm favourite at Old Trafford, and sister Tracey is also a sporting success story, having represented England at netball 74 times, winning the bronze medal at the 1998 Commonwealth Games in Kuala Lumpur. (♫ 'London Bridge Is Falling Down')

Gary Neville is a red
Is a red, is a red
Gary Neville is a red
He hates scousers

Philip Neville's still a red
Still a red, still a red
Phillip Neville's still a red
He hates scousers

Tracy Neville's off her head
Off her head, off her head
Tracy Neville's off her head
She plays netball

Neville Neville is their dad
Is their dad, is their dad
Neville Neville is their dad
His name's Neville

Celtic fans kindly sing to Andy Goram after press reports suggested the keeper was suffering from a mild form of schizophrenia: (♫ 'Guantanamera')

Two Andy Gorams
There's only two Andy Gorams!
Two Andy Gorams
There's only two Andy Gorams!

... and Brighton and Hove Albion fans enjoyed a similar chant following the marriage of their left-back Kerry Mayo to his new wife Kerry: (♫ 'Guantanamera')

Two Kerry Mayos
There's only two Kerry Mayos!
Two Kerry Mayos
There's only two Kerry Mayos!

Middlesborough fans enjoy the wordplay offered by the name of their striker Joseph Desire Job (and confront Teesside's unemployment record): (♫ 'Guantanamera')

One Job on Teesside
There's only one Job on Teesside!
One Job on Teesside
There's only one Job on Teesside!

It's clear how Arsenal fans spend their time, as they sing to Emmanuel Petit: (♫ 'Quartermaster's Store')

He's blonde
He's quick
His name's a porno flick
Emmanuel, Emmanuel!

They're clearly obsessed, as this is how they celebrate their strike force: (♫ 'Let's Talk About Sex')

Let's talk about Cesc baby
Let's talk about Flamini
Let's talk about Theo Walcott, Freddie Ljungberg and Henry
Let's talk about Cesc!

West Bromwich Albion find Black Country humour in the name of their Swiss defender: (♫ 'Blue Moon')

Bernt Haas
I've gone and Bernt my Haas!
I've gone and Bernt my Haas!
I've gone and Bernt my Haas!

And the Baggies fans find more fun in a name: (♫ 'Go West')

Bernt Haas
Shouldn't light his farts!
Bernt Haas
Shouldn't light his farts!

Just like Bernt Hass, Falkirk's French defender Cedric Uras really should have been warned before heading across the channel to Britain. Cedric only ever played nine games for Falkirk – I wonder why? (♫ 'England's Number One')

Cedric show us Uras!
Cedric, Cedric show us Uras!

Liverpool fans point out the obvious: (♫ 'Quartermaster's Store')

He's big
He's red
His feet stick out the bed
Peter Crouch, Peter Crouch!

He's tall
He's skinny
He can't fit in a mini
Peter Crouch, Peter Crouch!

From one extreme to the other and a trip to Brisbane Road, where the travelling fans of Brighton and Hove Albion celebrate a goal scored by midfielder Dean Cox. Cox stands at five foot four inches: (♫ 'Ta-Ra-Ra Boom-De-Ay')

We've got tiny Cox!
We've got tiny Cox!

Liverpool fans appreciate a looker: (♫ Lord of the Dance)

Dirk Kuyt, as good as he may be
Hit every branch on the ugly tree
Like Fowler, Crouch and Craig Bellamy
Dirk Kuyt's boss, but he's fucking ugly!

... and they also appreciate Jamie Carragher's dad! After Gary Carragher was banned from every ground in the country for being drunk while trying to enter a football ground, Liverpool fans wrote a suitable ode to their favourite central defender's father: (♫ 'Quartermaster's Store')

He's red
He's sound
He's banned from every ground
Carra's dad, Carra's dad!

Manchester United fans love their super-sub Ole Gunnar Solskjaer: (♫ 'You Are My Sunshine')

You are my Solskjaer, my Ole Solskjaer
You make me happy, when skies are grey
And Alan Shearer was fucking dearer
Oh please don't take my Solskjaer away!

On joining Middlesbrough, Fabrizio Ravanelli made the best possible debut. On the first day of the 1996/97 season, playing against Liverpool, Ravanelli scored a hat trick in a 3-3 draw. His trademark celebration spawned this song: (♫ 'Macarena')

We've got a player he's called Ravenelli
Scored three goals first time he was on the telly
After each goal he showed us his belly
Whoah Ravanelli!

Cardiff City pay tribute to their striker Nathan Blake and his allegedly chequered past: (♫ 'Quartermaster's Store')

He's black
He's mean
He robbed the fruit machines
Nathan Blake, Nathan Blake!

And another one from the City fans regarding their goalkeeper Mark Grew, who allegedly sold his FA Cup final tickets: (♫ 'Quartermaster's Store')

He's fat
He's stout
He is a ticket tout
Mark Grew, Mark Grew!

It's not an easy task to sing about your Polish forward when he goes by the name of Jackie Dziekanowski but Bristol City fans do their best: (♫ 'Hokey Cokey')

You put your left leg in
Your left leg out
In out, in out
You shake it all about
You do the Hokey Cokey and you turn around
That's what it's all about

Ooooooooooooh, Jackie Dziekanowski!
Ooooooooooooh, Jackie Dziekanowski!
Ooooooooooooh, Jackie Dziekanowski!

This Manchester City ditty followed the club buying their first Chinese player, the popular Sun Jihai: (♫ 'She'll Be Coming Round the Mountain')

Singing ay ay hippy Sun Jihai
Singing ay ay hippy Sun Jihai
Singing ay ay hippy
His dad's got a chippy
Singing ay ay hippy Sun Jihai

Cheltenham Town fans show their love for centre-back Gavin Caines and, in particular, his arse: (♫ 'I Love You Baby')

We love you Cainsey, your arse is super-sized
We love you Cainsey, you are our number 5
We love you Cainsey
Your nickname should be J-Lo

A local lad who captained Middlesbrough for over a decade, the tough centre-back Tony Mowbray was a hero on Teesside. Known as Mogga, he was was revered by 'Boro fans. Still, this song about catching people offside probably doesn't do him justice: (♫ 'Hokey Cokey')

Woah Tony Mowbray
Woah Tony Mowbray
Woah Tony Mowbray
Arm up, flag up, you're off side!

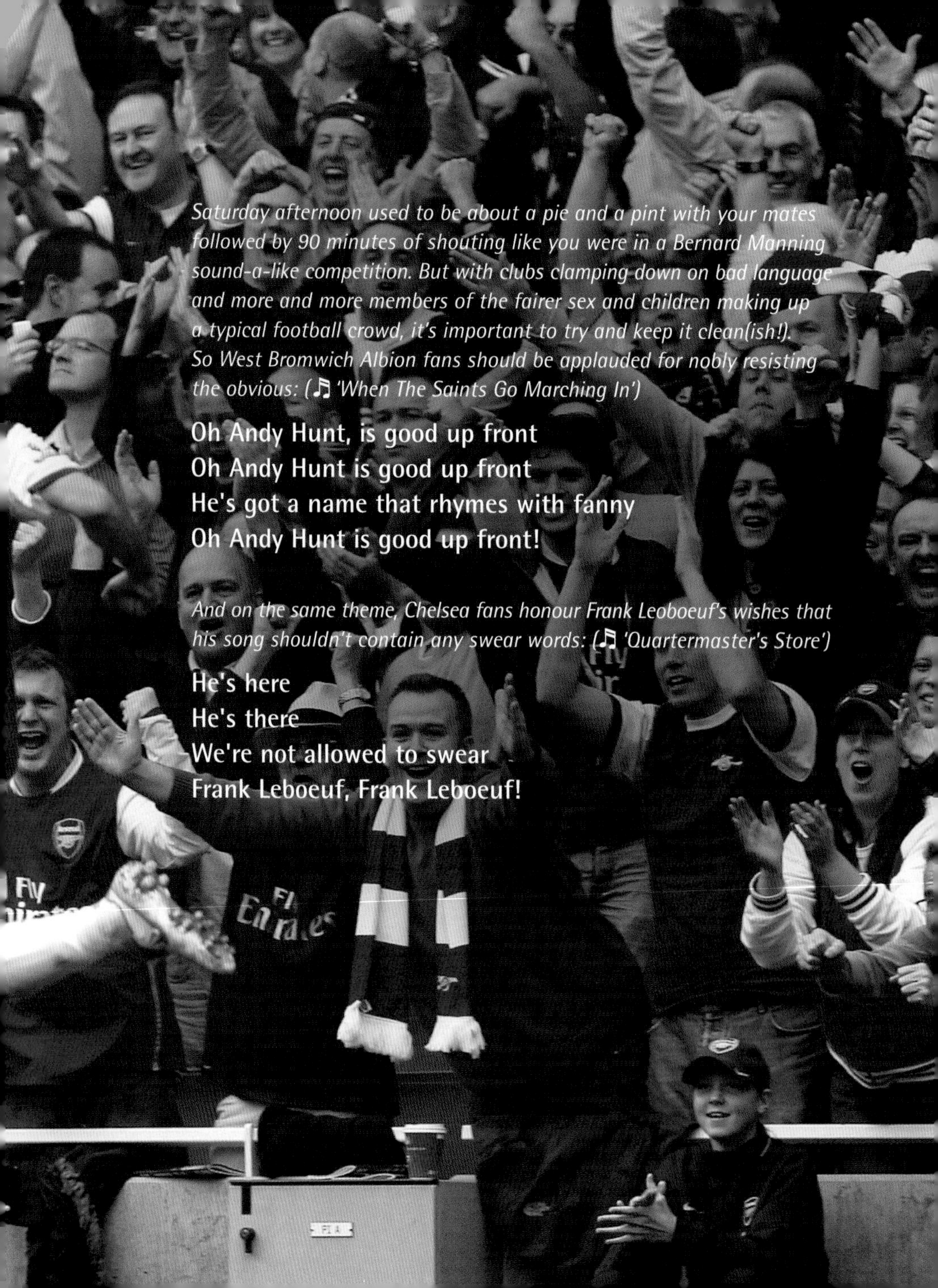

Saturday afternoon used to be about a pie and a pint with your mates followed by 90 minutes of shouting like you were in a Bernard Manning sound-a-like competition. But with clubs clamping down on bad language and more and more members of the fairer sex and children making up a typical football crowd, it's important to try and keep it clean(ish!). So West Bromwich Albion fans should be applauded for nobly resisting the obvious: (♫ 'When The Saints Go Marching In')

Oh Andy Hunt, is good up front
Oh Andy Hunt is good up front
He's got a name that rhymes with fanny
Oh Andy Hunt is good up front!

And on the same theme, Chelsea fans honour Frank Leoboeuf's wishes that his song shouldn't contain any swear words: (♫ 'Quartermaster's Store')

He's here
He's there
We're not allowed to swear
Frank Leboeuf, Frank Leboeuf!

Chelsea fans may love their French defender but the Wolves fans are clearly mad about their captain Gary Breen (and Steve Bull, of course): (♫ 'Yellow Submarine')

Number 1 is Gary Breen
Number 2 is Gary Breen
Number 3 is Gary Breen
Number 4 is Gary Breen
Number 5 is Gary Breen
Number 6 is Gary Breen
Number 7 is Gary Breen
Number 8 is Gary Breen
Number 9 is Stevie Bull
Number 10 is Gary Breen
Number 11 is Gary Breen
We all dream of a team of Gary Breens
A team of Gary Breens
A team of Gary Breens!

Cardiff City fans get all romantic with this ode to their striker Warren Feeney: (♫ 'You've Lost That Lovin' Feelin'')

We've got that Warren Feeney
Ooooh, that Warren Feeney!

An extensive buy-to-let property portfolio of almost 100 homes ensured Robbie Fowler's appearance on the 2005 Sunday Times *Rich List. It also led to this Man City chant: (♫ 'Yellow Submarine')*

We all live in a Robbie Fowler house
A Robbie Fowler house
A Robbie Fowler house!

While a modern-day Premier League player might expect to appear in the Times *Rich List, things are very different in the lower leagues of English football. So it's great to see fans of Southern League Division One South and West side Windsor and Eton FC helping to advertise for painter-and-decorator-cum-defender Dave Tilbury as he makes his 200th appearance for the club: (♫ 'Ta-Ra-Ra Boom-De-Ay')*

We've got Dave Tilbury
He'll paint your house for free
He quotes and estimates
He paints and decorates!

A few years ago, Pittodrie was home to two Moroccan internationals: Hicham Zerouali (known by the fans as Zero) and Rachid Belabed. The Aberdeen fans clearly enjoyed this African connection (or they just love The Quo!): (♫ 'Rockin' All Over the World')

Here we go and here we go and here we go
With Belabed and with Zero
Here we go
Moroccan all over the world!

(Hicham Zerouali was given the number 0 by Aberdeen in recognition of his nickname and popularity among the Aberdeen supporters. He represented his country 17 times, scoring three goals. He tragically died in a car accident in December 2004. Aberdeen retired the 0 shirt in his memory and he remains a firm favourite with fans of The Dons.)

In the summer of 2007, Newcastle signed Habib Beye from French side Marseille and he quickly became a favourite with the fans. Now I'm not sure if he has an office in a toilet or can start a juke box by clicking his fingers but heeeey, not everyone's as cool as the Fonz: (♫ 'Happy Days')

Sunday, Monday, Habib Beye
Tuesday, Wednesday, Habib Beye
Thursday, Friday, Habib Beye
Saturday, Habib Beye, rocking all week with you!

While on loan at Cardiff, Kasper Schmeichel, goalkeeper and son of Manchester United legend Peter Schmeichel, became a firm Ninian Park favourite. But all the saves in the world won't help when you're named after a ghost: (♫ 'Volare')

Kasper, Whoaoa
Kasper, Whoaoa
He stands between our posts
He's named after a ghost!

When striker Steve Lovell scores for Aberdeen against Hearts, the Don's fans break into voice à la Joy Division: (♫ 'Love Will Tear Us Apart')

Love, Lovell tear you apart, again.

THE PLAYERS YOU
LOVE TO HATE
2

For every great player your club signs, they're bound to find a dud. You know the one, the goalkeeper who can't catch, the defender who can't head a ball, the midfielder who runs like he's on 20 a day or the forward who couldn't hit a barn door from 10 yards. But while these players may not offer you much on the pitch, they offer a wealth of opportunities for the fans...

West Ham fans celebrate the shooting prowess of their striker Bobby Zamora: (♫ 'That's Amore')

When you're sat in Row Z
And the ball hits your head
That's Zamora!

Birmingham City fans send some Christmas cheer to their improving striker: (♫ 'Winter Wonderland')

There's only one Emile Heskey
One Emile Heskey
He used to be shite
But now he's all right
Walking in a Heskey wonderland!

And just so his spirits don't drop outside of the festive season, opposing fans give him some more support: (♫ 'She'll Be Coming Round the Mountain')

If Heskey plays for England, so can I!
If Heskey plays for England, so can I!
If Heskey plays for England
If Heskey plays for England
If Heskey plays for England, so can I!

When Pascal Cygan is brought in to cover for an injured player, Arsenal fans lend their support: (♫ 'Quartermaster's Store')

He's bald
He's shit
He gets a game when no one's fit
Pascal Cygan! Pascal Cygan!

Liverpool fans show their affection for defender Djimi Traore: (♫ 'Blame it on the Boogie')

Don't blame it on the Biscan
Don't blame it on the Hamann
Don't blame it on the Finnan
Blame it on Traore
He just can't, he just can't, he just can't control his feet!

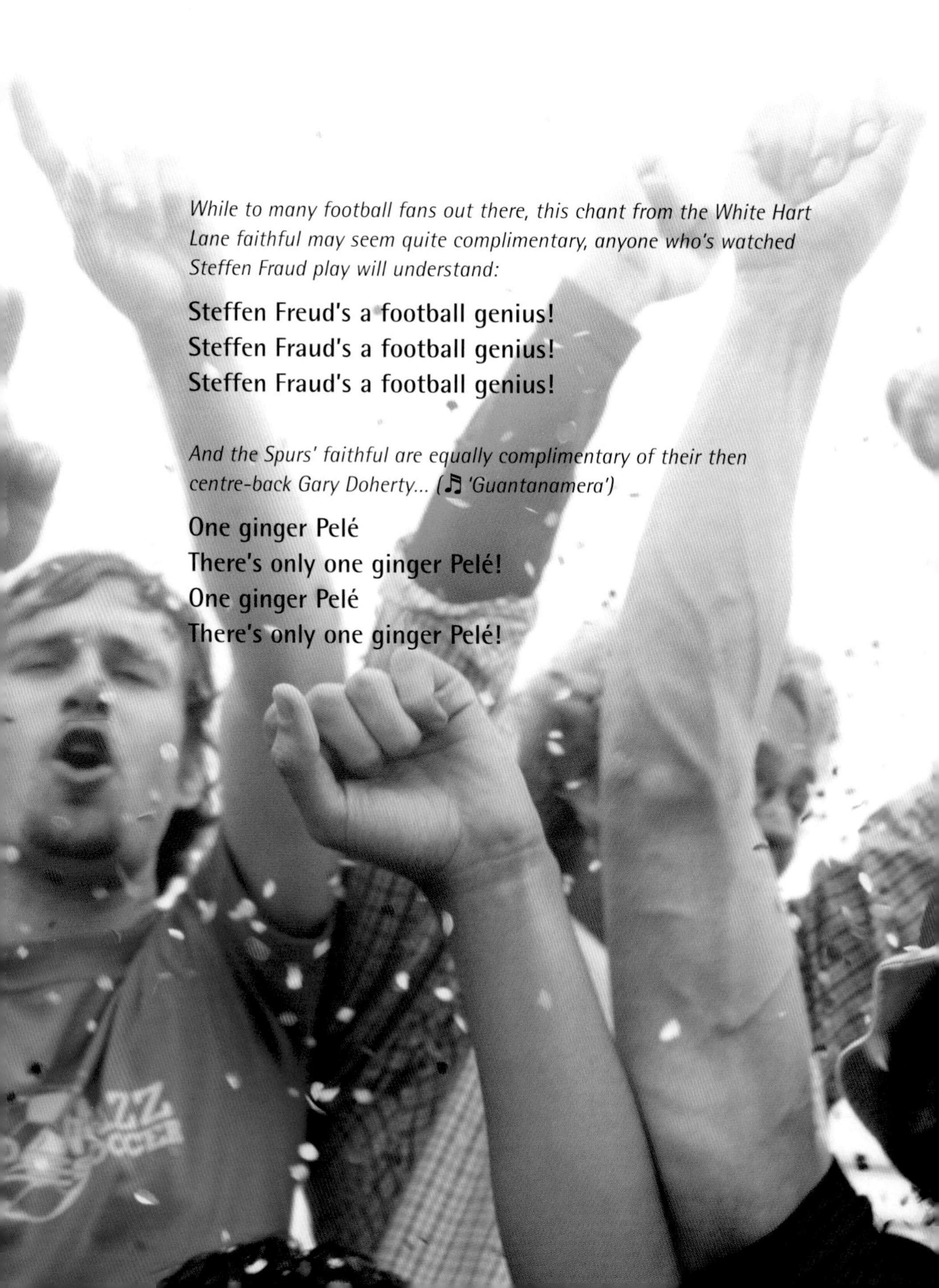

While to many football fans out there, this chant from the White Hart Lane faithful may seem quite complimentary, anyone who's watched Steffen Fraud play will understand:

Steffen Freud's a football genius!
Steffen Fraud's a football genius!
Steffen Fraud's a football genius!

And the Spurs' faithful are equally complimentary of their then centre-back Gary Doherty... (♫ 'Guantanamera')

One ginger Pelé
There's only one ginger Pelé!
One ginger Pelé
There's only one ginger Pelé!

Leading 2-0 against old firm rivals Celtic, the Rangers management decide to replace goal-scorer Kris Boyd (whose goal in the game was his 100th goal in the Scottish Premier League) with Filip Sebo (who only scored two goals in 32 appearances for Rangers). The decision prompted the Rangers fans to rejoice:

Sebo's on
We're taking the piss!
Sebo's on
We're taking the piss!

With only seven goals in 88 appearances for Chelsea, Jesper Gronkjaer was never as effective as his talent suggested he should be. But if he didn't exactly light up the Premier League, he did at least give fans the chance to sing Bon Jovi: (♬ 'Living on a Prayer')

Oooooh he's got blonde hair
Oooooh Jesper Gronkjaer!
Pass him the ball, he'll fuck up I swear
Oooooh Jesper Gronkjaer!

WHO ATE ALL THE PIES?

3

They might not always be of the same ilk as Vinnie Jones or Robbie Savage, but's there's always someone in the opposing 11 who you just don't like. It may be that you would love him if he played for your team, but he doesn't – so you don't! Whether they tackle like a man possessed, or left your club to move across town to your closest rivals, they just wind you up. They're the pantomime villain to your panto crowd, and so naturally your job is to make sure that you boo, hiss and generally ridicule the player at every opportunity.

Not satisfied with 'Who ate all the pies?', Rangers fans decide to taunt Celtic's vertically challenged John Hartson with a more biblical tune: (♫ 'All Things Bright and Beautiful')

All things bright and beautiful
All creatures great and small
All things wise and wonderful
John Hartson ate them all!

Goalkeeper Jerzy Dudek's penalty shoot-out heroics helped Liverpool to their fifth Champions League Trophy in 2005. No wonder the away fans try to put him off: (♫ 'Quartermaster's Store')

It's big
It's thick
It's bigger than his dick
Dudek's nose!
Dudek's nose!

Evertonians were delighted when Liverpool's top striker Ian Rush left Liverpool and the English League to sign for Juventus. Relieved that they would no longer be on the wrong end of a Rush goal in a Merseyside derby, the Everton fans sang with great delight: (♫ the traditional Liverpudlian folk song 'Maggie May')

Oh, Ian, Ian Rush is off to Juventus
And he won't play at Anfield anymore, anymore
Oh we all think it's funny that he has took the money
And he won't play at Anfield anymore!

... and often followed it up with: (♫ 'Chirpy Chirpy Cheep Cheep')

Where's your Rushie gone?
Where's your Rushie gone?

(Ian Rush re-signed for Liverpool in 1989 and in the FA Cup final that year came off the bench to score two goals, as Liverpool won 3-2 in extra time against, yes, you guessed it, Everton! Never count your chickens too soon!)

Millwall fans make a subtle change to the traditional 'You're supposed to be at home', to give some stick to the diminutive Northampton left-back Danny Jackman: (♫ 'Guide Me O Thou Great Redeemer')

You're supposed to be a gnome!

While Bishops Stortford fans seize on the opportunity to adapt the Toni Basil classic when they're 2-0 up against St Albans (whose keeper is conveniently called Nick Eyre): (♫ 'Mickey')

Hey Nicky you're so fine, you're so fine, you're two behind
Hey Nicky!

Fans at Sittingbourne carry this little ditty in their arsenal, perfect for any player who makes a bad mistake: (♫ 'When the Saints Go Marching In')

My niece of two (my niece of two)
Is better than you (is better than you)
My niece of two is better than you
She's got a doll and a pushchair
My niece of two is better than you!

A vote on the BBC website to find the most popular chant of the 2006/07 season showed the nation's favourite was sung by the Liverpool fans during a match with Barcelona. Directed at two-times winner of the FIFA World Player of the Year award, Ronaldinho: (♫ 'Conga')

Cilla wants her teeth back
Cilla wants her teeth back
La la la la, la la la la!

Now if I've learnt anything from going to the football, it's that anyone with a pun in their name is in for some real stick. Enter Colchester goalkeeper Dean Gerken, who comes in for some unwanted attention from both the Crystal Palace fans... (♫ 'Guantanamera')

Stayed in a burger
You should have stayed in a burger!
Stayed in a burger
You should have stayed in a burger!

and (♫ 'Ta-Ra-Ra Boom-De-Ay')

Your dad's a cucumber! Your dad's a cucumber!

... and the Liverpool fans during a pre-season friendly: (♫ 'Guantanamera')

Small nasty pickle
You're just a small nasty pickle!
Small nasty pickle
You're just a small nasty pickle!

Liked in McDonalds
You're not even liked in McDonalds!
Liked in McDonalds
You're not even liked in McDonalds!

(At six foot four I'm not sure how many of the Palace or Liverpool fans would say that to his face!)

And while we're on keepers getting jip, the former QPR number 1 Lee Camp should probably not expect anything more high brow than this chant from the Leyton Orient fans: (♬ 'Go West')

You're Camp
And you know you are!
You're Camp
And you know you are!

The Torquay fans enjoy their 4-2 victory over Stevenage Borough and especially the fact that Stevenage keeper Alan Julian had appeared (at least to the home fans) to have scored two own goals: (♬ 'Conga')

Keeper's on a hat-trick
Keeper's on a hat-trick
La la la la, la la la la!

(For the record only one of Torquay's four were credited to Julian.)

And just to prove that being a goalkeeper can be the loneliest of jobs, Barnet's number 1 Lee Harrison has to endure the sarcastic taunts of the Norwich City fans after their side takes a 5-0 lead within 31 minutes against The Bees: (♬ 'England's Number One')

England's Number One!
England's England's Number One!

And if it's sarcasm you're after, look no further than the Sheffield Wednesday fans, who, with the score at 5-0, chant to Southampton keeper Kelvin Davis: (♫ 'England's Number One')

Davis give us a save
Davis, Davis give us a save!

But we all know it's not just the man between the posts who comes in for some stick. Any player whose footballing school report would read 'should do better' is bound to take some flak. So when Ipswich's Dan Harding puts a free kick over the bar and into the top tier of Portman Road's south stand, the Ipswich supporters show their fine rugby voices: (♫ 'Swing Low, Sweet Chariot')

Swing low, sweet chariot
Coming for to carry me home
Swing low, sweet chariot
Coming for to carry me home!

And not to be outdone, the Wolves supporters join in with the fun... (♫ 'Guantanamera')

One Jonny Wilkinson
There's only one Jonny Wilkinson!
One Jonny Wilkinson
There's only one Jonny Wilkinson!

Birmingham City fans enjoy an uncharacteristic poor performance from the West Brom striker Kanu: (♫ 'She'll Be Coming Round the Mountain')

I'd rather have a speedboat than Kanu
I'd rather have a speedboat than Kanu
Yes I'd rather have a speedboat
Rather have a speedboat
Rather have a speedboat than Kanu!

I'd rather have a raft than Kanu
I'd rather have a raft than Kanu
Yes I'd rather have a raft
Rather have a raft
Rather have a raft than Kanu!

Now I'd rather fucking drown than have Kanu
Now I'd rather fucking drown than have Kanu
Yes I'd rather fucking drown
Rather fucking drown
Rather fucking drown than have Kanu!

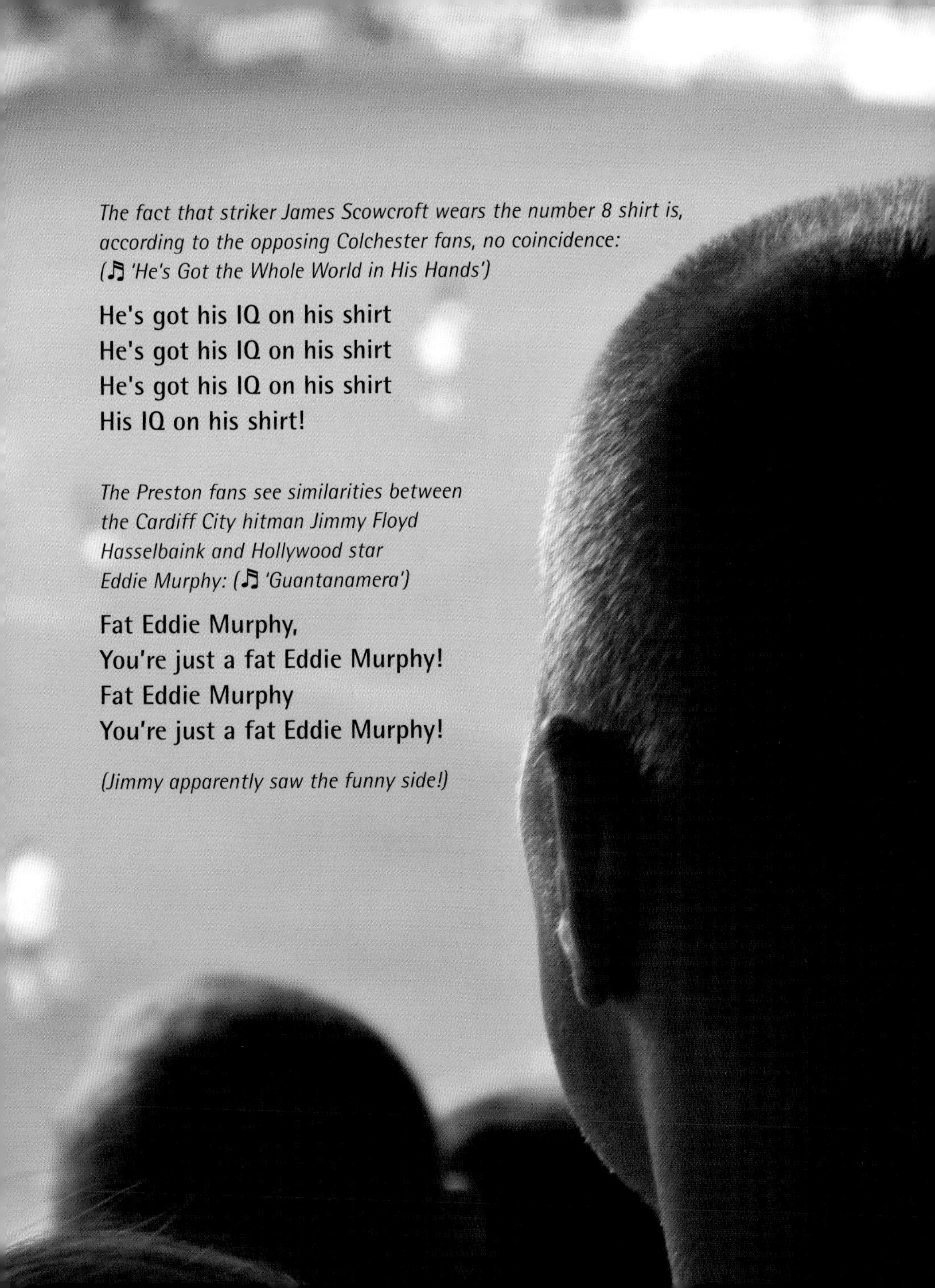

The fact that striker James Scowcroft wears the number 8 shirt is, according to the opposing Colchester fans, no coincidence: (♫ 'He's Got the Whole World in His Hands')

He's got his IQ on his shirt
He's got his IQ on his shirt
He's got his IQ on his shirt
His IQ on his shirt!

The Preston fans see similarities between the Cardiff City hitman Jimmy Floyd Hasselbaink and Hollywood star Eddie Murphy: (♫ 'Guantanamera')

Fat Eddie Murphy,
You're just a fat Eddie Murphy!
Fat Eddie Murphy
You're just a fat Eddie Murphy!

(Jimmy apparently saw the funny side!)

THE
MANAGERS
4

He picks the best side, buys the greatest players and sells the ones who just don't make the grade. He is a master tactician who can inspire the team with rousing 'Once more unto the breach'-type speeches and, when things aren't going your way, he makes one of those inspired substitutions that change the game. Well at least that's what you hope he does!

When your manager is as good as you'd hope he's adored and you sing his name home and away. But for every Bill Nicholson there's a Graeme Souness, for every Sir Alf Ramsey there's a Gordon Strachan and for every Sir Alex Ferguson there's a Christian Gross! It's time to celebrate the good, the bad and the ugly of the football management world...

Everton fans show they're an 'open-minded' bunch; they're even happy having a ginger at the helm:

Davey Moyes, Davey Moyes
Davey Davey Moyes
He's got red hair
But we don't care
Davey Davey Moyes!

During a 5-1 thrashing at the hands of Middlesbrough, the Bolton striker El Hadji Diouf was sent off for foul and abusive language. Knowing how Big Sam Allardyce can react to such situations the 'Boro fans tried to wind him up: (♬ 'Guantanamera')

Whinge on the telly
He's going to whinge on the telly!
Whinge on the telly
He's going to whinge on the telly!

(To his credit Big Sam actually said of the game and the red card, 'I've no complaints about the score – we got exactly what we deserved – or the red card.' Maybe the chant made a difference?)

Gary Johnson twice signed defender Liam Fontaine, first for Yeovil Town and then for Bristol City. While clearly a fan of the player, he apparently didn't rate his goal-scoring abilities and, in an interview with Bristol City World, declared that 'Fonts will never score: if he does I will show my backside in Burton's window.' This throwaway comment was seized upon and the gauntlet thrown down by Johnson was reported in the Bristol Evening Post *and the* Western Daily Press *and led to a Soccer AM 'I want Liam to score' campaign. T-shirts were made and the progress of City's defender was avidly followed by fans across the nation. Inevitably, on his 108th professional appearance away at Wolves, Liam scored, sparking the ecstatic City fans to sing: (♫ 'England's Number One')*

Johnson, show us your ass!
Johnson Johnson, show us your ass!

... and also: (♫ 'Conga')

Gary get your ass out
Gary get your ass out
La la la la, la la la la!

While at Christmas time, the City fans sing an ode to their manager: (♫ 'Santa Claus is coming to town')

He got us up once
He'll get us up twice
He'll get his arse out, it's not very nice
Gary Johnson's coming to town!

When Gordon Strachan took over at Southampton, the Pompey fans gave their opinion on the manager of their south coast rivals (any excuse to sing a bit of Gloria Gaynor!): (♫ 'I Will Survive')

At first I was afraid, I was petrified
Thought I'd never get a another job with a premiership side
And I spent so many nights, thinking I'd done nothing wrong
But I grew strong
And a new job came along...

And so I'm back, managing the Saints!
They think I'm gonna save them, but it's obvious I ain't
They should have called on Howard Wilko, Harry R or Georgie G
If they want a decent gaffer, then it sure as hell ain't me!

But I'll survive, I will survive
As long as I've mates on telly, I know I'll stay alive!
The new Saints boss job is mine, and I've crap players yet to sign
I will survive, I will survive!

Go on now go, walk out the door
They'll be singing at St. Mary's, when we're in division four
But it'll be nothing to do with me
My team weren't strong mentally
But now I got a big fat pay-off
And my country's calling me...

So I'll survive, I will survive!
I'll take Scotland to the World Cup
With Hansen by my side
We'll get beaten by Cameroon
Sent home after just round one
But I'll survive!
I will survive!
Hey hey!

(Quickly followed by dancing in the stands of Fratton Park!)

Gordon Strachan gets off lightly in comparison with the former Liverpool captain Phil Thompson. Here's just a few of the songs directed at poor Phil as he directed his teams from the sidelines: (♫ 'Bread of Heaven')

Get your nostrils
Get your nostrils
Get your nostrils off the pitch!
Get your nostrils off the pitch!

(♫ 'Guantanamera')

Sneeze in a minute
He's gonna sneeze in a minute!
Sneeze in a minute
He's gonna sneeze in a minute!

(♫ 'He's Got the Whole World in His Hands)'

He's got the whole world in his nostrils
He's got the whole wide world in his nostrils
He's got the whole world in his nostrils
He's got the whole world in his nostrils!

I'm not sure he would have ever got so much support from the England fans but Manchester City's revival under Sven-Goran Eriksson has endeared him to the Eastlands faithful – so much so that they're offering their wives as an incentive: (♫ 'Lord of the Dance')

Sven, Sven, wherever you may be
You are the boss of Man City
You can shag my wife
On our settee
If we win the cup at Wembley!

... and many City fans claim Sven's already 'acquainted' with their other half: (♫ 'She'll Be Coming Round the Mountain')

If Sven has shagged your wife, clap your hands! [clap clap]
If Sven has shagged your wife, clap your hands! [clap clap]
If Sven has shagged your wife, Sven has shagged your wife
If Sven has shagged your wife, clap your hands! [clap clap]

From one former international manager to another, and the now infamous story of Niall Quinn's disco pants. The original song began life following a Manchester City pre-season tour to Italy in 1992. A bust-up with team-mate Steve McMahon had led to Niall removing his bloodied shirt. Later in the evening, a topless Quinn was dancing wearing just a pair of cut-off jeans. Unbeknownst to the future Sunderland chairman, a group of Man City fans were watching and by the end of the evening were serenading their then-player with this new chant: (♫ 'Here We Go')

Niall Quinn's disco pants are the best
They go up from his arse to his chest
They're better than Adam and the Ants
Niall Quinn's disco pants!

When Quinn moved to the northeast and Sunderland, The Mackems fans adopted the song and it was even released as a single by the Sunderland fanzine A Love Supreme *in April 1999 – the single reached number 59 in the UK singles chart, at which point you would have thought the story of Niall's disco pants would end. But oh no, there's more. Following an away win at Cardiff, a group of joyous Sunderland fans spotted their chairman at the airport and began singing 'Niall Quinn's Disco Pants'. They carried on chanting as they got on the plane, causing so much disruption that eventually the plane was delayed so long it missed its take-off slot. This left Mr Disco Pants himself, some of the Sunderland staff, and the fans stranded miles away from home. So Niall, true to the heroic reputation he has on Wearside, coughed up the cash to pay for taxis home for all of the Sunderland supporters, a gesture that has since led to a variation on the song being heard at the Stadium of Light... (♫ 'Here We Go')*

Niall Quinn's taxi cabs are the best
So shove it up your arse Easyjet!
Fat Fred wouldn't do it for the Mags
Niall Quinn's taxi cabs!

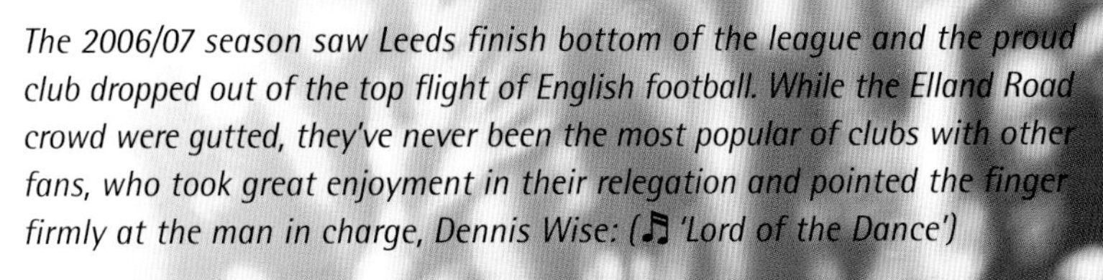

The 2006/07 season saw Leeds finish bottom of the league and the proud club dropped out of the top flight of English football. While the Elland Road crowd were gutted, they've never been the most popular of clubs with other fans, who took great enjoyment in their relegation and pointed the finger firmly at the man in charge, Dennis Wise: (♫ 'Lord of the Dance')

Wise Wise whatever have you done?
You've taken Leeds to division one
You won't win a cup, you won't win a shield
and your biggest game will be Huddersfield!

... and as if poor Dennis Wise hadn't had enough, the Wolves fans put the boot in: (♫ 'Guantanamera')

One Jimmy Krankie
There's only one Jimmy Krankie!
One Jimmy Krankie
There's only one Jimmy Krankie!

The 'Forward with Franny' campaign sought to see former playing hero Francis Lee take over as Manchester City chairman from the increasingly unpopular Peter Swales. In 1994, Lee did indeed take over as chairman but the club's fortunes on the pitch did not improve and City were relegated from the Premier League in 1996. In the following season, the City fans who had made the journey south to Loftus Road expressed their disappointment with the lack of direction the club was showing under Francis Lee, chanting 'Bring back Peter Swales'. This was a particularly scathing attack on the club's boardroom staff, given that Peter Swales had died in May of that year, a fact that didn't deter the rather morbid City fans who continued with: (♫ 'Here We Go')

Dig him up, dig him up, dig him up!

During a six-year reign at Hull City, former manager Terry Dolan twice guided the Tigers to relegation. Naturally the Hull fans weren't too enamoured with Terry... (♫ 'Common People')

He came from Rochdale with a lack of knowledge
He studied management at Bradford College
That's where I... caught his eye
He told me that he was a manager
I said: 'In that case you'd better come and manage us'
He said: 'Fine'
And then, in three seasons' time
He said: 'I want to take you to the Vauxhall Conference!
I want to do whatever Halifax do!
I want to sign lots of shitty players
I want to watch this club slide out of view
And hoof and hoof and hoof
Because...
There's nothing left to do!

But let's not finish this chapter on such a clever re-working of an anthemic song. Instead, let's leave it to the Liverpool supporters who spring into song whenever manager Rafa Benítez asks substitute Dirk Kuyt to start warming up: (♫ 'Conga')

Rafa's got his Dirk out
Rafa's got his Dirk out
La la la la, la la la la!

THE FANS

5

Football is nothing without the fans, and so it's no surprise that some of the best songs are odes to ourselves, or, more often than not, abuse to be thrown at the opposition fans. Especially when your team are playing poorly, some well-aimed insults allow you to take pride in the fact that at least you're better fans than the other lot...

Both Millwall and Leeds fans tell it like it is: (♫ 'She'll Be Coming Round the Mountain')

We're the best behaved supporters in the land
We're the best behaved supporters in the land
We're the best behaved supporters, best behaved supporters
Best behaved supporters in the land... when we win!

Pause

We're a right set of bastards when we lose
We're a right set of bastards when we lose
We're a right set of bastards, right set of bastards
Right set of bastards... when we lose!

... and the Millwall faithful have been known to add a third verse:

We're completely non-committal when we draw
We're completely non-committal when we draw
We're completely non-committal, completely non-committal
We're completely non-committal... when we draw!

When told they couldn't stand up at Middlesbrough, Manchester City fans responded in suitably cheeky fashion: (♫ 'Go West')

Stand up
'Cos they said sit down!
Stand up
'Cos they said sit down!

Chelsea fans are simple in their abuse of the FC Bruges supporters: (♫ 'Go West')

You're French and you know you are!
You're French and you know you are!

... and adapt a classic terrace chant especially for the visiting fans from the Turkish club Galatasaray: (♫ 'Go West')

You're Shish
And you know you are!
You're Shish
And you know you are!

Newcastle fans take national stereotypes one step further when they take the lead against Swiss side FC Basle: (♫ 'Guide Me O Thou Great Redeemer')

You're not yodelling
You're not yodelling
You're not yodelling anymore!
You're not yodelling anymore!

But just to prove that English football fans are as happy with stereotypes closer to home, here's a favourite one sung by the away fans visiting Anfield: (♫ 'You Are My Sunshine')

You are a scouser
An ugly scouser
You're only happy on giro day
Your mum's out thieving
Your dad's drug dealing
Oh please don't take my hubcaps away!

The Liverpool contingent get more stick... (♫ 'You'll Never Walk Alone')

Sign on, sign on
With a pen in your hand
Cause you'll never get a job!

And while we're on a roll: (♫ 'Hey Baby')

Heeeeeeeey scousers oh ah
I wanna knoooooow where's my video? (and my stereo, and my DVD)

Why stop there? When Manchester City were enjoying a 5-0 victory against Everton shortly before Christmas in 2000 they put a twist in the usual 'you should have gone Christmas shopping' chant: (♫ 'Guantanamera')

Gone Christmas robbing
You should have gone Christmas robbing!
Gone Christmas robbing
You should have gone Christmas robbing!

Okay, just one more, sung by the Hammers to Liverpool: (♫ 'Ta-Ra-Ra Boom-De-Ay')

We've got Di Canio
You've got our stereo!

Moving away from Liverpool, and West Ham fans show sympathy towards the Ipswich supporters during the 2001 foot and mouth crisis: (♫ 'Chirpy Chirpy Cheep Cheep')

Where's your cattle gone?
Where's your cattle gone?

And another one reserved for taunting fans from rural areas is the Millwall chant: (♫ 'Head, Shoulders, Knees and Toes')

Head, shoulders, foot and mouth, foot and mouth!

A classic sung by many, but often to Norwich: (♫ 'The Addams Family')

Your sister is your mother
Your father is your brother
You all fuck one another
The Norwich Family!

The well-researched Nottingham Forest fans remind Hartlepool that the town is most famous for the hanging of a monkey during the Napoleonic wars:

E-I-E-I-E-I-O – a monkey-hanging you will go!

And the Stockport County fans are equally well educated: (♫ 'Frère Jacques')

Go to Burnley
Go to Burnley
Take some rope
Take some rope
It's a town of monkeys
It's a town of monkeys
They're all French
They're all French!

Of the many chants aimed at un-vocal opposition support, none are quite as caring as the Portsmouth fans: (♫ 'Go West')

Don't sing
Or you'll wake them up!
Don't sing
Or you'll wake them up!

Nottingham Forest met Chelsea in the fourth round of the FA Cup in the 2006/07 season. The Forest fans have had to endure turbulent times in recent years but their fans are faithful, at least more so, they would claim, than their west London opponents: (♫ 'Bread of Heaven')

Where were you
Where were you
Where were you when you were shit?
Where were you when you were shit?

Tottenham fans change a classic Chelsea song to reflect the modern-day visitor to Stamford Bridge: (♫ 'Lord of the Dance')

Carefree wherever you may be
We are the nouveau Chelsea FC
So please sit down
So my wife can see
I've been coming here since 2003!

Almost every London team had a good laugh at Tottenham's expense following the events of the final day of the 2006 season. Going into the final match, Spurs needed to win away at West Ham in order to secure the lucrative fourth Champions League spot. However, ten players fell ill after contracting food poisoning, apparently from lasagne. Tottenham failed to beat the Hammers, allowing bitter rivals Arsenal to claim the fourth place and Champions League qualification: (♫ 'That's Amore')

When the Spurs start to cry
When they don't qualify
Blame lasagne
When they think it's a treat
But it's really dodgy meat
Blame lasagne!

West Ham fans rub it in some more: (♫ 'Volare')

Lasagne, Whoaoa
Lasagne, Whoaoa
We laughed ourselves to bits
When Tottenham got the shits!

A quick delve into the world of international football chants reveals the imaginative threat made by Scottish fans to their Italian counterparts: (♫ 'Guantanamera')

Deep fry your pizzas
We're gonna deep fry your pizzas!
Deep fry your pizzas
We're gonna deep fry your pizzas!

And the Aberdeen fans in Madrid prove that pizzas aren't the only food they can give the Scottish treatment to: (♫ 'Guantanamera')

Deep fry your tapas
We're gonna deep fry your tapas!
Deep fry your tapas
We're gonna deep fry your tapas!

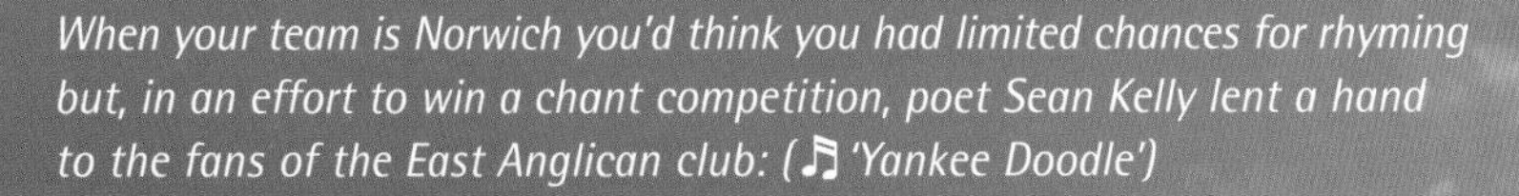

When your team is Norwich you'd think you had limited chances for rhyming but, in an effort to win a chant competition, poet Sean Kelly lent a hand to the fans of the East Anglican club: (♫ 'Yankee Doodle')

Delia Smith's a brilliant cook
She feeds our whole team porridge
She makes a cracking steak au poivre
But that don't rhyme with Norwich!

Chorus:
We don't care and we're all right
You're a bunch of fairies
We're the Kings of Carrow Road
We are the Canaries!

Robbie Green's so brave and true
He's well known for his courage
Naturally there is just one
Club for him, and that's Norwich!

Darren Huckerby is great
He's always on the forage
He'd really like to score some goals
But that don't rhyme with Norwich!

The famous chant contest is here
We wish we'd been to college
We didn't, so we didn't learn
More words to rhyme with Norwich!

But steak au poivre isn't to everyone's taste so Norwich fans start making requests... (♫ 'Cecilia')

Delia, You're breaking my heart
You're baking a tart, for us daily
Oh Delia, I'm down on my knees
I'm begging you please, make parmos. Make parmos!

Norwich may have Delia as a celebrity fan, but Arsenal fans manage to find the humour in newspaper reports that they have a somewhat less enviable supporter, Osama Bin Laden: (♫ 'Volare')

Osama, Whoaoa
Osama, Whoaoa
He supports the Arsenal
He's hiding near Kabul!

Osama, Whoaoa
Osama, Whoaoa
He comes from Taliban
He is an Arsenal fan!

If newspaper reports are to be believed, Osama Bin Laden isn't the only avid follower of the Arsenal. Reports in the tabloids suggested that the Queen, following in her mother's footsteps, is in fact a Gooner. I hope for the sake of the nation that this is untrue but, if nothing else, the stories did lead to this great version of our national anthem: (♬ 'God Save the Queen')

God save our gracious Queen
She loves the Arsenal team
God save our Queen!
Da da da da
She fucking hates West Ham
Chelsea and Tottenham
She is a Gooner through and through
God save our Queen!

Many fans know that a smidgen of geographic artistic license is a great way to belittle the opposing fans. This one was sung to Leeds fans: (♬ 'Guantanamera')

Small town in Bradford
You're just a small town in Bradford!
Small town in Bradford
You're just a small town in Bradford!

And Arsenal fans are among many who taunt Chelsea with: (♬ 'Guantanamera')

Shit team in Fulham
You're just a shit team in Fulham!
Shit team in Fulham
You're just a shit team in Fulham!

While most fans take these geographic inaccuracies just a little further when playing Walsall: (♫ 'Guantanamera')

Small town in Poland
You're just a small town in Poland!
Small town in Poland
You're just a small town in Poland!

But it's important to remember that some geography is relative. Hence a song usually reserved for teams hailing from north of Birmingham can be equally well used by the Pompey faithful when playing a combative Watford side:

You dirty northern bastards!
You dirty northern bastards!

Some fans are better with their geography than others and getting lost on your way to and from an away ground is par for the course for travelling fans. But you're especially likely to come a cropper on your way to see your team play against Rushden and Diamonds. The Diamonds play their home games at Nene Park in the small Northamptonshire town of Irthlingborough, the smallest town in England to have been home to a football league team. It's no wonder the Barnsley fans got lost: (♫ 'When The Saints Go Marching In')

I've no idea (I've no idea)
How to get home (How to get home)
I've no idea how to get home
We're in the middle of nowhere
I've no idea how to get home!

To this day I can't quite work out why the Norwich fans, directing this chant at their bitter rivals from Ipswich, saw this as offensive: (♫ 'Guantanamera')

Town not a city
You're a town not a city!
Town not a city
You're a town not a city!

... and I'm not sure exactly how many of the Nottingham Forest crowd the Oldham fans thought they would offend with this one, but at least it's funny: (♫ 'She'll Be Coming Round the Mountain')

If Robin Hood was real, he'd be dead
If Robin Hood was real, he'd be dead
If Robin Hood was real
If Robin Hood was real
If Robin Hood was real, he'd be dead!

Newcastle fans enjoy a wee tipple... (♫ 'Lord of the Dance')

Drink, drink, wherever we may be
We are the drunk and disorderly
And we will drink wherever we may be
For we are the drunk and disorderly!

I was drunk last night
I was drunk the night before
And I'm gonna get drunk like I've never been drunk before
'Cos when we're drunk, we're as happy as can be
For we are the drunk and disorderly!

They're either masters of irony up in Barnsley or completely blind. We'll give them the benefit of the doubt: (♫ 'Blue Moon')

Brazil, it's just like watching Brazil
It's just like watching Brazil
It's just like watching Brazil!

Leeds turned this chant on its head when coming back from 2-0 down to take a 3-2 lead against Barnsley at Oakwell: (♫ 'Blue Moon')

Ryhl, it's just like watching Ryhl
It's just like watching Ryhl
It's just like watching Ryhl!

Last winning the league in 1961 can only lead to Tottenham getting some abuse from Arsenal: (♫ 'When the Saints Go Marching In')

You won the league (you won the league)
In black and white (in black and white)
You won the league in black and white
You won the league in the sixties
You won the league in black and white!

While the fortunes of the two North London clubs have differed in recent years, neither have faired as badly as Leeds United. The passionate Leeds fans have had to endure being relegated twice in the last four years to leave them in the third tier of English football. But their sense of humour has never left them, and with the prospect of playing in the Johnstone's Paint Trophy the Leeds followers keep their eyes on the prize:

Wembley, Wembley
We're the famous Leeds United and we're off to win some paint
Wembley, Wembley!

Luton fans are an incredibly honest bunch, and there's no denying why they're watching Luton against Cardiff City on Valentine's Day: (♫ 'Guantanamera')

Here 'cos we're single
We're only here 'cos we're single!
Here 'cos we're single
We're only here 'cos we're single!

The Tottenham fans who chose to travel to the Czech Republic on Valentine's Day, to see their team's 2-1 victory against Slavia Prague, ensure that their loved ones back home understand their priorities:

I love Tottenham more than you!

... and just so they're in no doubt:

You can stick your fucking roses up your arse!

Bristol City fans give their opinion of their Welsh rivals from across the Severn Estuary: (♫ 'Hokey Cokey')

Woooooh, Cardiff City
Woooooh, Cardiff City
Woooooh, Cardiff City
Knees bent, arms stretched
Chav Chav Chav!

... while fans of Inverness Caledonian Thistle are only slightly more subtle in their abuse of the Ross County supporters: (♫ 'The Wheels On the Bus')

The wheels on your house go round and round
Round and round
Round and round
The wheels on your house go round and round
All day long

It's not often that you can abuse rival fans on two counts with just one song, but Preston North End fans manage it with this chant directed at a particularly portly Millwall fan, who is part of a rather low attendance at The New Den: (♫ 'Knees Up, Mother Brown')

Who ate all the fans?
Who ate all the fans?
You fat bastard, you fat bastard
You ate all the fans!

Low attendances are always a great excuse for away fans to give the lack of home support some stick and, away at Southend, that's exactly what Barnsley fans do: (♫ 'Quartermaster's Store')

They're here
They're there
They're every-fucking-where
Empty seats, empty seats!

And when the attendance is somewhat limited by the size of the ground, the Villa fans sing: (♫ 'When the Saints Go Marching In')

My garden shed (my garden shed)
Is bigger than this (is bigger than this)
My garden shed is bigger than this!
It's got a door, and a window
My garden shed is bigger this!

The smallest stadium in the Championship is Colchester's Layer Road. With a capacity of just 7,556 it's dwarfed by many of the stadiums in the league, including the Valley, home of Charlton. Still, it is perhaps a little unfair that the travelling Charlton fans enquire: (♫ 'Bread of Heaven')

Is your ground from
Is your ground from
Is your ground from B&Q?
Is your ground from B&Q?

Oldham Athletic fans take advantage of the pun offered to them by their clubs name...

Give us a T (T!)
Give us an I (I!)
Give us a T (T!)
Give us an S (S!)
What do you do with 'em?
Old'um! Old'um!

Although they are known locally as The Gas, Bristol Rovers' official nickname is The Pirates. It's only natural that the Stockport County fans might enquire as to why: (♫ 'She'll Be Coming Round the Mountain')

Why are you called The Pirates?
Why are you called The Pirates?
Why are you called The Pirates?
'cos you arrrrrrhhhh!

Liverpool fans show sympathy (of sorts) to their counterparts from Inter Milan: (♫ 'Show Me the Way to Go Home')

Show them the way to go home
They're tired and they wanna go to bed (for a wank!)

With 58 letters, Llanfairpwllgwyngyllgogerychwyrndrobwllllantysiliogogogoch is the longest officially recognized place name in the UK. With the pronunciation of the village's name as hard as its spelling, few fans, other than those from Wrexham and a handful of other Welsh clubs, would even contemplate singing this one: (♫ 'Guide Me O Thou Great Redeemer')

Are you Llanfairpwllgwyngyllgogerychwyrndrobwllllantysil-iogogogoch in disguise?
Are you Llanfairpwllgwyngyllgogerychwyrndrobwllllantysil-iogogogoch in disguise?

After taking a 4-0 lead against Plymouth, following a barren spell that saw Burnley go 18 games without a win, fans of The Clarets begin to question which team it is they're watching: (♫ 'Guide Me O Thou Great Redeemer')

Are you Burnley in disguise?
Are you Burnley in disguise?

... and a bit later, they still struggle to comprehend what's going on: (♫ 'Guide Me O Thou Great Redeemer')

What the fuck is going on?!
What the fuck is going on?!

Fans of Blue Square Premier side Histon question whether the particularly short referee would feel more at home in Middle Earth: (♫ 'Guide Me O Thou Great Redeemer')

Are you Frodo in disguise?

In the Scottish Cup, Airdrie United striker Allan Russell's shot bounced off the cross bar and onto the goal line. Claims the ball had crossed the line were waved away, but maybe the piss-taking Kilmarnock fans got a better view: (♫ 'Here We Go')

That was in, that was in, that was in!

Your team is 2-0 down in the 82nd minute and you're praying for a miracle. Well, for fans of Worcester City that miracle happened, in the form of a partial floodlight failure that caused their game with Nuneaton Borough to be abandoned. I think we can all appreciate how the Worcester contingent felt as they chanted to the Nuneaton fans: (♫ 'Bread of Heaven')

We can't see you
We can't see you
We can't see you sneaking out!
We can't see you sneaking out!

Sadly for Aberdeen, a brief floodlight failure away at Hearts proved to be only a temporary reprieve as they were thumped 4–1. But the game wasn't all bad for the travelling fans as they enjoyed the opportunity for fun offered by the blackout: (♫ 'Guide Me O Thou Great Redeemer')

Have yeh no paid yer
Have yeh no paid yer
Have yeh no paid yer 'leccy bill?
Have yeh no paid yer 'leccy bill?

Since 2003, Newcastle United have been sponsored by the bank Northern Rock, whose head offices are based in the city. But with the 2007 credit crisis and subsequent nationalization of the bank the Derby fans can't help but have some fun at the Toon Army's expense: (♫ 'Guantanamera')

Banked with The Woolwich
You should have banked with The Woolwich!
Banked with The Woolwich
You should have banked with The Woolwich!

Following a 3-2 defeat at the hands of QPR, Luton Town's manager Mike Newell felt aggrieved that the officials (referee Andy D'Urso and assistant referee Amy Rayner) had failed to award Luton a penalty. QPR defender Marcus Bignot had tangled with Luton's Trinidadian winger Carlos Edwards in the penalty area and the Luton manager was convinced a spot kick should have been given. In a post-match interview Newell said of assistant referee 'She should not be here. I know that sounds sexist, but I am sexist, so I am not going to be anything other than that.' While the incident landed Newell with a £6,500 FA fine, the Luton fans took their manager's new reputation in their stride:

Mike Newell's Sexist Army!
Mike Newell's Sexist Army!

... and in a game against Derby, when a refereeing decision doesn't go their way:

The referee's a woman!
The referee's a woman!

When a rather rotund Preston supporter started shouting, the Leeds contingent pounced, even managing to use a song by local band and United fans the Kaiser Chiefs: (♫ 'I Predict a Riot')

I predict a diet, I predict a diet!

GREAT COMEBACKS

6

There's nothing better when you're taking some flack than a witty retort to silence the opposition fans. Points are awarded for speed of reply and severity of put down. Bonus points for a bit of self-depreciation and singing back in the same tune, just to show the adaptability of your song repertoire...

Prior to their 2003 UEFA Cup final against Seville, the Celtic fans taunt their Old Firm rivals:

You'll be watching 'The Bill', when we're in Seville!

... but a week later, following Celtic's cup final defeat, Rangers fans reply in sympathetic style:

We were watching 'The Bill', what was the score in Seville?

When Carlisle United take the lead against League One rivals Swansea, their fans are in party mood: (♫ 'Conga')

Let's all have a disco
Let's all have a disco
La la la la, la la la la!

... but late in the match two goals in two minutes give Swansea a 2-1 victory and put the Welsh fans in gate-crashing mood: (♫ 'Conga')

Let's go to their disco
Let's go to their disco
La la la la, la la la la!

As the half time scores are read out at Bramall Lane, the mention over the Tannoy of arch rivals Sheffield Wednesday's name causes the United fans declaration that:

We hate Wednesday
And we hate Wednesday
We hate Wednesday
And we hate Wednesday
We hate Wednesday
And we hate Wednesday
We are the Wednesday haters!

...Man City fans respond with:

We hate Saturday
And we hate Saturday
We hate Saturday
And we hate Saturday
We hate Saturday
And we hate Saturday
We are the Saturday haters!

(If you're losing away to Sheffield United who wouldn't hate Saturdays?)

The chant from the Hillsborough regulars of:

Wednesday till I die
I'm Wednesday till I die
I know I am
I'm sure I am
I'm Wednesday till I die!

... is greeted by the Wolves fans, who, clearly possessing a dark sense of humour, point out the obvious:

It's Wednesday tomorrow
It's Wednesday tomorrow
I think it is
I'm sure it is
It's Wednesday tomorrow!

When beating Arsenal, West Ham fans were keen to point out that they were doing so despite having lost a man to an earlier sending-off: (♫ 'Blue Moon')

10 men, we've only got 10 men!

... Arsenal fans, though, were quick to point out West Ham's point's tally: (♫ 'Blue Moon')

10 points, you've only got 10 points!

... and when Liverpool were just as quick to highlight the uneven sides, the Man United faithful responded in equally scathing fashion: (♫ 'Blue Moon')

10 pence, you've only got 10 pence!

With Delia Smith being a majority shareholder at Norwich, Chelsea fans goad their Norwich counterparts with: (♫ 'Guantanamera')

One Gordon Ramsey
There's only one Gordon Ramsey!
One Gordon Ramsey
There's only one Gordon Ramsey!

... but Norwich fans are quick to respond with the differences between the Chelsea Russian billionaire owner Roman Abramovich and their Delia: (♫ 'Ta-Ra-Ra Boom-De-Ay')

You've got a Russian crook, we've got a super cook!

... However, following her eccentric outburst at one recent Norwich match, Chelsea fans reply: (♫ 'Ta-Ra-Ra Boom-De-Ay')

We've got Abramovich, you've got a crazy bitch!

Newcastle fans taunt Manchester City after signing the former Blues star: (♫ 'Conga')

We've got Joey Barton
We've got Joey Barton
La la la la, la la la la!

... but when City go into a 3-1 lead, they reply in equally ecstatic fashion: (♫ 'Conga')

You've got Joey Barton
You've got Joey Barton
Ha ha ha ha, ha ha ha ha!

Playing against northeast rivals Sunderland, the Newcastle fans reel out the old staple for when you're playing a team who are struggling at the foot of the table: (♫ 'Here We Go')

Going down, going down, going down!

... to which the Sunderland fans quickly sing back: (♫'Here We Go')

So are we, so are we, so are we!

Swindon fans enjoy the humiliation of Gillingham as their side leads 5-0: (♫ 'Go West')

You're shit
And you know you are!
You're shit
And you know you are!

... but the Gillingham support is nothing if not honest: (♫ 'Go West')

We're shit
And we know we are!
We're shit
And we know we are!

As their team begins to provide a real threat to the Liverpool defence, Sheffield Wednesday fans urge their team on:

Come on Wednesday, Come on Wednesday!

... which is cheekily misinterpreted by the Liverpool fans:

Why, is it Giro day? Oh why, is it Giro day?

Chelsea fans, enjoying their club's recent wealth, taunt their London rivals Arsenal: (♫ 'Guide Me O Thou Great Redeemer')

Shall we buy a
Shall we buy a
Shall we buy a ground for you?
Shall we buy a ground for you?

... forgetting that, sadly, Arsenal haven't got a bad record in the league: (♫ 'Guide Me O Thou Great Redeemer')

Shall we win the
Shall we win the
Shall we win the league for you?
Shall we win the league for you?

'We've won it five times' is a Liverpool classic celebrating their club's great achievement of winning the European Champions League five times. I'm not sure how many of them would have expected this superb response from the Wigan faithful: (♫ 'Sloop John B')

We've won it two times
We've won it two times
AutoWindscreen
We've won it two times!

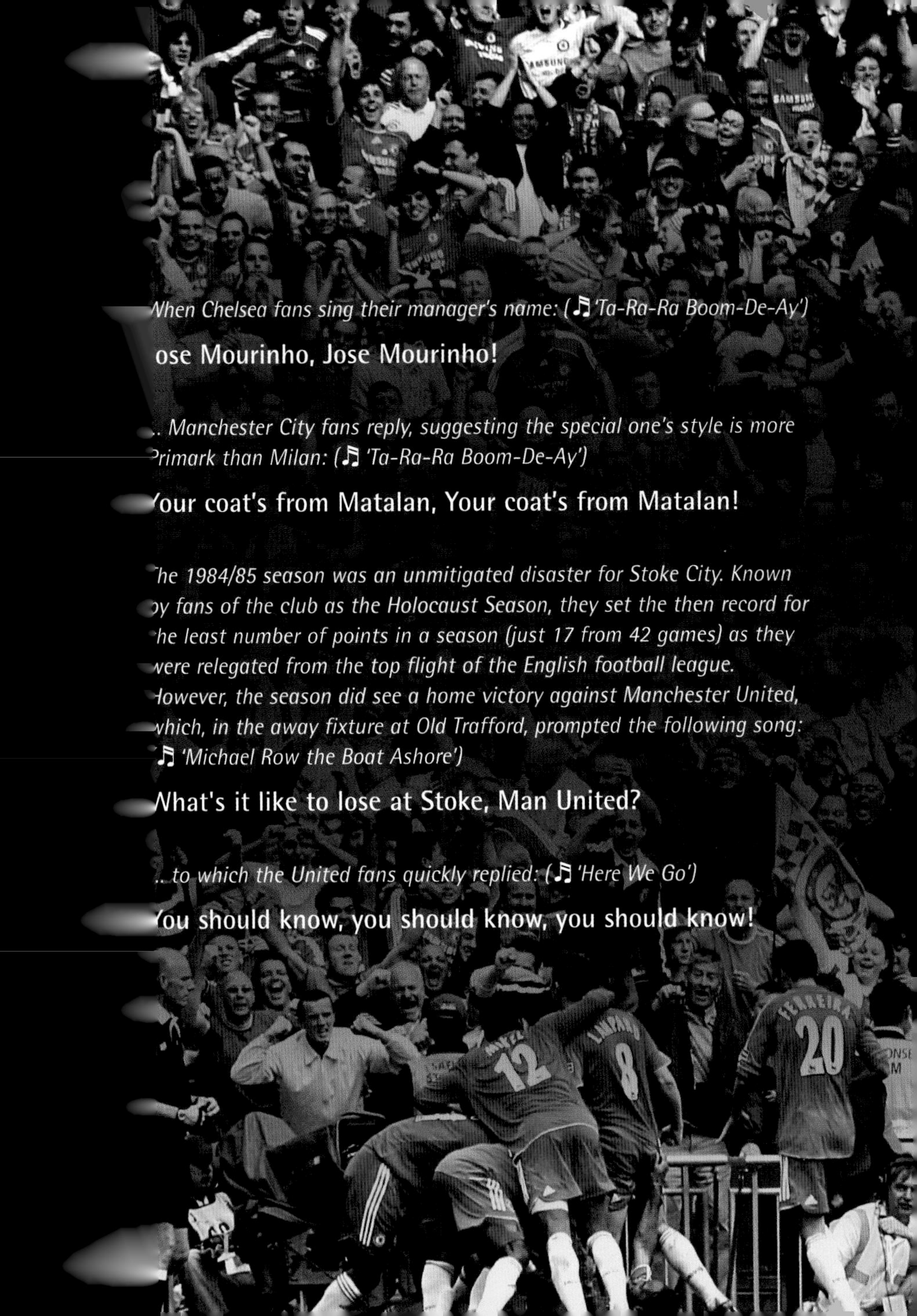

When Chelsea fans sing their manager's name: (♫ 'Ta-Ra-Ra Boom-De-Ay')

ose Mourinho, Jose Mourinho!

.. Manchester City fans reply, suggesting the special one's style is more Primark than Milan: (♫ 'Ta-Ra-Ra Boom-De-Ay')

Your coat's from Matalan, Your coat's from Matalan!

The 1984/85 season was an unmitigated disaster for Stoke City. Known by fans of the club as the Holocaust Season, they set the then record for the least number of points in a season (just 17 from 42 games) as they were relegated from the top flight of the English football league. However, the season did see a home victory against Manchester United, which, in the away fixture at Old Trafford, prompted the following song: (♫ 'Michael Row the Boat Ashore')

What's it like to lose at Stoke, Man United?

.. to which the United fans quickly replied: (♫ 'Here We Go')

You should know, you should know, you should know!

Ever wondered who that bloke is who stands at the back of the stand banging a drum? Well Sheffield United fans do and so they sing: (♫ 'Guide Me O Thou Great Redeemer')

Who's the wanker?
Who's the wanker?
Who's the wanker with the drum?
Who's the wanker with the drum?

... and poor Sam really knows who his friends are when the other Colchester fans reply: (♫ 'Guide Me O Thou Great Redeemer')

Sam's the wanker
Sam's the wanker
Sam's the wanker with the drum
Sam's the wanker with the drum!

At 0-0 the Bradford fans are confident of securing passage into the next round of the Carling Cup: (♫ 'Que Sera')

Que sera sera
Whatever will be will be
We're going to Wembley
Que sera sera!

... but when Wolves score two goals in the first four minutes of the second half, the dream crumbles: (♫ 'Que Sera')

Que sera sera
Whatever will be will be
We're going to Shrewsbury
Que sera sera!

The Exeter fans, when the referee's decisions during the first 45 minutes don't exactly go their way, sing:

The referee's a wanker!

... and while it might not strictly speaking be a comeback, the Exeter fans' reply to their own chant when they are awarded two second-half penalties shows how fickle us football fans can be:

The referee's a legend!

Hampden Park in Glasgow played host to the 2002 Champions League Final. Manchester United were knocked out of the competition in the semi-finals by eventual runners-up Bayer Leverkusen. While in the competition the United fans proudly sang: (♫ 'The Entertainer')

United are going to Glasgow
Follow, follow, follow
'Cos United are going to Glasgow
There'll be thousands of Reds
We'll be pissed out our heads
'Cos United are going to Glasgow!

... Manchester rivals City took the song and made it more appropriate to their then Championship status: (♫ 'The Entertainer')

City are going to Tesco
Follow, follow, follow
'Cos City are going to Tesco
There'll be thousands of blues
Queuing for booze
'Cos City are going to Tesco!

Wimbledon's victory at Selurst Park over Stockport County was County's 28th defeat of the 2001/02 campaign and saw them relegated from Division One. But rather than be dismayed, the Stockport County fans decide to celebrate with the 'Relegation Conga': (♫ 'Conga')

The Relegation Conga
Division One no longer
La la la la, la la la la!

... and when the stewards stop the snaking conga for 'ground safety' reasons, the Stockport fans, back in their seats, sing: (♫ 'Conga')

The Stationary Conga
The Stationary Conga
La la la la, la la la la!

WE'RE SHIT AND
WE KNOW WE ARE!
7

Sometimes in life, things just don't go your way: missing out on that perfect promotion, bumper-to-bumper traffic on the way to the ground or finding out that your new girlfriend is an Arsenal fan. And like in life, football can be cruel. But when things are against you on the football pitch (which is actually quite often, if you're a Spurs fan!) then you can always fall back on a touch of gallows humour...

Carlisle United fans face the unenviable position of only seeing their team score once in five consecutive games: (♫ 'We'll Meet Again')

We'll score again
Don't know where, don't know when
But I know we'll score again some sunny day!

During the 90th minute of the match, in the final game of the season, and with their side losing 2-1, Bradford fans face up to their team's inevitable relegation with just a hint of Yorkshire wit: (♫ 'Guantanamera')

Down in a minute
We're going down in a minute!
Down in a minute
We're going down in a minute!

And again, when Bradford fans find themselves in the final minutes of a 3-0 defeat at home to Accrington Stanley (who the hell are they? Exactly!), they react with a little bit of make believe: (♫ 'Guide Me O Thou Great Redeemer')

Let's pretend
Let's pretend
Let's pretend we've scored a goal!
Let's pretend we've scored a goal!

(Followed by all the fans celebrating wildly!)

Against Everton, Bolton fans hand out the abuse and admit their own shortcomings, all in seven words: (♫ 'Go West')

We're shit
But you're worse than us!
We're shit
But you're worse than us!

West Bromwich Albion fans refuse to admit they're no good but instead have a novel approach to reading the league table: (♫ 'When the Saints Go Marching In')

The premier league (the premier league)
Is upside down (is upside down)
The premier league is upside down
We're up the top and Chelsea the bottom
The premier league is upside down!

... followed shortly by:

Champions, Champions, Champions!

By contrast, the fans of Boston United are not at all deluded about their club's position but are just as proud: (♫ 'Go West')

We're cheats
And we know we are!
We're cheats
And we know we are!

Losing 3-0 away at Preston North End, the Stockport County fans never lose faith:

Four-three
We're gonna win four-three!

At 4-0 down...

Five-four
We're gonna win five-four!

When Preston score their fifth...

Six-five
We're gonna win six-five!

But when Preston's sixth goes in, the Stockport fans are slightly more realistic: (♫ She'll Be Coming Round the Mountain)

If you'd settle for a point, clap your hands! [clap clap]
If you'd settle for a point, clap your hands! [clap clap]
If you'd settle for a point, settle for a point
If you'd settle for a point, clap your hands! [clap clap]

NOTHING
TO DO?
8

We've all been there, watching a nil-nil bore draw between two mid-table teams who couldn't pass a ball for toffee. So when it's more like watching a pub team than a top team, Brentford than Brazil, and you can't taunt the opposition supporters any more, then it's time to turn your attention to, well, anyone!

Sung to the local constabulary when they're policing a game:

'The Bill'! It's just like watching 'The Bill'!

Chelsea fans to a group of St John Ambulance volunteers:

You're going home in a speeding ambulance!

... and their London counterparts Crystal Palace also turn the song on its head. The South London club ran a promotion whereby children could get into certain games for a pound, the promotion being aptly titled 'Kid for a quid'. This evidently led to a large proportion of one home gate being made up of children, sparking the older Palace fans to sing:

You're going home in a Fisher Price ambulance!

While an attractive female St John Ambulance nurse sparks the Bolton fans to declare:

I'm going home in a St John's ambulance!

On a trip to Gay Meadow for the FA cup tie against Shrewsbury, the Chelsea supporters turn their vocal attention to a male streaker:
(♫ 'Bread of Heaven')

Is that all she
Is that all she
Is that all she gets at home?
Is that all she gets at home?

Former 'Coronation Street' star Thomas Craig played the mechanic Tommy Harris in the soap for three years. The character was murdered by his daughter who, in a fit of rage, hit him over the head with a wrench. When Thomas Craig was spotted in the crowd at a Heart of Midlothian game the Hearts fans blurred the lines between fiction and reality: (♫ 'Guantanamera')

Killed in a garage
You got killed in a garage!
Killed in a garage
You got killed in a garage!

I never would have thought that Corrie would have inspired so many football chants but the Hearts fans are clearly not alone in following the goings-on on the street. West Ham fans taunt the Manchester City faithful away at Eastlands: (♫ 'Here We Go')

Vera's dead, Vera's dead, Vera's dead!

A dog running onto the pitch at St Andrews caused the Barnsley fans to rather harshly chant: (♫ 'Guantanamera')

One Karen Brady
There's only one Karen Brady!
One Karen Brady
There's only one Karen Brady!

A half-time marriage proposal at a Cambridge United game leads to the followers of The U's giving the husband-to-be some support: (♫ 'Conga')

We've all had your missus
We've all had your missus
La la la la, la la la la!

And in a similar vein, the appearance of a bride and groom at The Valley ground led to the travelling Coventry fans giving the happy couple some pre-marital advice: (♫ 'Guantanamera')

Know what you're doing
You don't know what you're doing!
Know what you're doing
You don't know what you're doing!

The Manchester United megastore at Old Trafford is huge, selling everything from United Christmas decorations to football shaped TVs, babies' bibs to United garters (is there anything less likely to put you in the mood?). So the United fans decided to pay homage to their club's megastore and its huge array of products: (♫ 'My Old Man's a Dustman')

Oh the megastore is magic, they sell some magic hats
And when I saw the duvet, I said 'I'm having that'!
I even bought the curtains, and dressing gown in white
I follow Man United, 'cos they sell a load of shite!

I'm not sure what the visiting fans made of the Villa Park faithful chanting:

Take your shoes off if you love Villa!

(Followed by the fans taking their shoes off and waving them about!)

But for possibly the most random chant of them all we have to look no further than the fans of Hearts. Not satisfied with singing at soap stars, they turn their attention to really important matters... condiments. At an away game where the ground only served salt and vinegar with chips, the Hearts fans let their feelings be known: (♫ 'Blue Moon')

Brown sauce
We only like brown sauce
We only like brown sauce
We only like brown sauce!

Once they've got their sauces sorted, the Hearts supporters turn their attention to their keeper Steve Banks. Leading 4-1 against Aberdeen, they can afford to chant: (♫ 'England's Number One')

Banksy swing on the bar!
Banksy, Banksy swing on the bar!

(At which point Banks obligingly ran up and swung on the cross bar!)

Maybe random chants are an Edinburgh speciality, as the Hibs fans have also been known to sing slightly unusual songs. Take this one, sung to Queen of the South fans, whose team are based in Dumfries close to the English border. Apparently you're unable to get a Channel 4 signal there: (♫ 'Bread of Heaven')

Have you ever?
Have you ever?
Have you ever seen 'ER'?
Have you ever seen 'ER'?

Acknowledgments

I owe a huge amount to the following people for their help in putting this book together. Thanks to:

My brother, David, for his tireless help in contacting unofficial fan clubs to ask for their funniest songs, his help wading through the responses, his suggestion for the title of this book, his great sense of humour and his advice on the first draft.

My editor (and sister!), Kate, for all her support and encouragement, and for helping me with my spelling. And to my other sister, Rose, so she isn't left out – even though she did nothing of any use!

My girlfriend, Lynn, for replying to countless e-mails while I was off swanning around the world and for putting up with me constantly singing rude songs around the house for the last two months.

Sean Kelly for kindly allowing me to use his great Norwich chant on page 59. You can read more of Sean's poetry at www.kellywit.com.

Last but by no means least, thanks to everyone who has sent in their favourite songs and chants. The response has been phenomenal and if anyone finds this book in the slightest bit amusing it's all down to those fans who took the time and made the effort to contact me with the best from their club's fans. In particular I would like to thank the followng people for their contribution: Roly Allen, Neil Andrews, Paul Bowen, Sean Cable, Steve Callaghan, Alex Channon, David Chatterton, Chix, St. John Cox, Matt Davies, Marie Day, John Donovan, Patrick Ebbutt, Jonathan Fear, Tom Fisher, David Ford, Daniel Francis, Matt Gabb, Adam Grimshaw, Graham Houtby, Paul Howarth, Graeme Howlett, Bill Hunter, Brendan Kemp, Matt Ladson, Brian Lancaster, Phil Lines, Phil Loynd, Davie Macintosh, Jon Marshall, Johnny Martin, Dave Moore, Andy Morgan, Daniel Munn, Dan Oakes, Steve Parish, Heidi Pickup at Man City Info Via The Alps, Mark Redgrave, Rug, Rob Quinlan, Charles Sinclair, Nick Tompkins, Geoff Vickers, Tom Vickers, Anthony Ward, Ian Warburton, and everyone who contributed via barnsleyfc.org.uk, No Idle Talk, pne-online.co.uk and ziderheads.co.uk.

Thanks to the following for allowing their images to be used in this book: page 6 © Colin McPherson/Corbis; page 14 © iStock/Ronnie Wu; page 18 © Tommy Hindley/NewSport/ Corbis; page 20 © iStock/Paul Morton; pages 26–27 © Turba/zefa/Corbis; page 30 © Eddie Keogh/Reuters/Corbis; page 32 © iStock/Jim Jurica; page 33 © iStock/Cathleen Clapper; pages 36–37 © iStock/Marcus Lindström; page 45 © Geoff Caddick/epa/Corbis; page 47 © Ben Radford/Corbis; page 57 © iStock/Franco di Meo; pages 58–59 © Leo Mason/Corbis; page 67 © iStock/Mark Barnes; page 74 © iStock/Andy Medina; page 80 Andy Rain/epa/Corbis; page 86 © iStock/Gary Martins; page 95 © iStock/Slobo Mitic